D0672540

# I Just Want To Talk To You, Beetle Bailey

by
Mort Walker

# I Just Want To Talk To You, Beetle Bailey

by
Mort Walker

tempo
books

GROSSET & DUNLAP
A FILMWAYS COMPANY
Publishers • New York

6-2

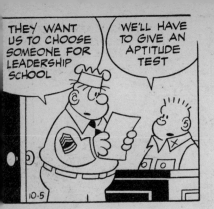

6-28

4-19

4-14

MORT
WALKER

WOULDN'T IT BE EASIER
JUST TO WASH THEM,
INSTEAD OF MAKING
SURE THEY
HAVEN'T BEEN
USED?